How-To Guides for Fier...

A Shogun Guide

Thanks to the creative team:
Senior Editor: Alice Peebles
Consultant: John Haywood
Fact Checker: Kate Mitchell
Design: www.collaborate.agency

Hungry Tomato™
A division of Lerner Publishing Group, Inc.
241 First Avenue North
Minneapolis, MN 55401 USA

For reading levels and more information, look up this title at
www.lernerbooks.com.

Main body text set in Blokletters Balpen 9/13.
Typeface provided by LeFly Fonts.

Library of Congress Cataloging-in-Publication Data

Names: Chambers, Catherine, 1954- author.
Title: A shogun's guide / Catherine Chambers.
Description: Original edition. | Minneapolis : Hungry Tomato, 2017. | Series:
How-to guides for fiendish rulers | Audience: Ages 8 to 12. | Includes index.
Identifiers: LCCN 2016021982 (print) | LCCN 2016027407 (ebook) | ISBN
9781512415520 (library bound : alkaline paper) | ISBN 9781512430745
(paperback : alkaline paper) | ISBN 9781512427080 (eb pdf)
Subjects: LCSH: Shoguns—History—Juvenile literature. | Japan—Kings and
rulers—History—Juvenile literature. | Japan—History—1185-1868—Juvenile
literature. | Japan—Social life and customs—1185-1600—Juvenile literature.
| Japan—Social life and customs—1600-1868—Juvenile literature.
Classification: LCC DS837 .C33 2017 (print) | LCC DS837 (ebook) | DDC
952/.02—dc23

LC record available at https://lccn.loc.gov/2016021982

Manufactured in the United States of America
1-39912-21382-8/10/2016

How-To Guides for Fiendish Rulers

A Shogun's Guide

by Catherine Chambers
Illustrated by Ryan Pentney

HUNGRY
TOMATO.

CONTENTS

Writing Down My Rules

I am an utterly fiendish shogun. I have ruled Japan with an iron fist. But I am getting older. My son will become shogun when I die. Only tough rules will keep him in power. So I have decided to write them down to help him be as fiendish as me.

MY RULES MUST BE WRITTEN CLEARLY.
The royal scribes shuffle in, bowing before me. Their hands clasp lacquered writing boxes, the *suzuri-bako*. Each scribe picks up an ink stick. He grinds it around a well made of traditional ink stone. He adds water and dips in his fine weasel-hair brush.

"Stop!" I shout. One of the scribes is using a wolf-hair brush. It will totally spoil the effect. I feel quite faint. My courtier sends for the doctor.

MY SUBJECTS MUST TELL ME THE TRUTH. The doctor hurries in. He is also my royal Buddhist priest. I ask him how long I have got. Will my rules be written before I die? He tells me that my body is in chaos. There is a bad spirit inside me.

"Get it out!" I order. He is very calm and recites sutras, Buddhist texts. Then he gives me some green tea. Is that it? My samurai guards drag the useless doctor away.

I INSIST ON THE BEST. My new doctor is an expert in our traditional *kampo* medicine. He tells me my blood is poor and gives me a drink of cinnamon and hoelen mushroom. Then he says I must have needle treatment, or acupuncture. That's better. The doctor mentions I will need many long needles. The scribes look pleased. They care about me. The doctor first burns a lot of moxi herb. Its fumes waft over my body. Then he picks up his needles. Fabulous. Maybe I will live long after all.

The scribes have written my rules. They put down their brushes. The ink has dried on their sheets of finest washi bark paper. I glow with pride. My chief scribe collects the sheets. The rules look amazing. My work is done. I hope my son will be grateful for them. OR ELSE!

How I Became Shogun

I am the fearless military ruler of Japan. I followed very strict rules to get to the top, like all shoguns since the twelfth century. Now I make the rules for everyone else. I always wear expensive silk kimonos and carry a carved ivory fan and ceremonial dagger. You cannot miss me.

It's a hard life making rules, as you can see.

Kyoto

Edo

NO OTHER RULER IS ALLOWED TO OVERPOWER ME. My people fear me, but I would like them to show some respect. They often think more highly of the emperor than of ME. This is because he is the cultural leader of Japan, and a god. The truth is, he handed power down to me. So I owe him, which is very annoying.

Nobody likes me? See if I care!

I FOLLOWED THE RULES TO BECOME SHOGUN.

I am the son of a mighty shogun. I am also a warlord and a first-class warrior. My family has run the country for many generations. But we always have to keep an eye on other powerful families. They might take over. Of course, a long time ago, my ancestors overpowered a ruling family to install their own shogun. I think that was fair. After all, we protect Japan from foreign invaders.

I'll learn all Dad's rules, then we can take over.

I MUST NOT BE WEAK.

I have always been a ruthless, disciplined, and brave warrior, skilled in strategy and cunning. I follow the example of my hero, Minamoto Yoritomo (1147-1199), the first shogun. He improved the way that the country was run and increased Japan's wealth. Good organization across the whole land helped him stay in power. This meant that shoguns could keep military control over Japan. Very good news for ME!

Fiendish Fact File

- *Shogun* means "a general who subdues barbarians."

- Shoguns ruled Japan between the twelfth and nineteenth centuries. The first shogun, Minamoto Yoritomo, ruled from 1192 to 1199.

- Oda Nobunaga (1534-1582) gained power by using European firearms. He burned temples and killed innocent civilians.

Somehow I don't think they'll be returning.

THE EMPEROR MUST NOT RISE AGAINST ME.

It is very difficult for me to rule while the emperor sits in his palace in Kyoto City. I watch him closely from my capital, Edo, in case he forms a powerful army. Worse, he could encourage another military commander to take the title shogun. Terrifying.

My Rules on Religion

Our ancient Shinto faith is very powerful in Japan. So I have to think carefully before I make rules about it. Many of my subjects believe that the emperor is the son of the Shinto sun goddess, Amaterasu. This could make life very difficult for me. Hmmm.

I BLEND TWO RELIGIONS. There would be a national riot if I got rid of Shintoism. Instead, I just reduce its importance. Since the twelfth century, shoguns like me have favored a type of Buddhism called Zen. But I am clever enough to include Shinto traditions in our temples. I follow the shogun who blended Buddhist and Shinto practices in Kamakura City's most important temple. This was a smart rule. It pleased all those subjects who are still fond of the emperor.

I FOLLOW ZEN BUDDHIST RULES. I expect my officials, generals, and warriors to follow them too. It is most important to meditate and perform controlled exercises every day. These actions give me a clear mind and awaken my inner spirit. I must not confuse my thinking with a spider's web of meaningless words. That rule helps all my subjects.

I thought this was the Shogun's favorite temple.

Maybe he wanted the melted gold.

MY BUDDHIST TEMPLES MUST BE SENSATIONAL. They show power over Shintoism and ME above the Emperor. My favorite temple is Rokuon-ji, the Golden Pavilion in Kyoto. It was first built in the 1390s. But we shoguns and our enemies have burned it down many times. Those are the rules of war, I'm afraid.

I USE MY TEMPLES AS A WEAPON. My warriors sometimes unite against me. So I use the temple schools to educate a strong merchant class to balance them. Merchants increase the wealth of the nation too. If they get too powerful, I can always overcome them.

Fiendish Fact File

- Zen Buddhism came from India and spread to China in the sixth century. It reached Japan by the twelfth century, when shoguns were taking over.

- By the middle of the seventeeth century, there were temple schools across Japan. They taught reading, writing, abacus, morals, and European languages.

- Shoguns felt threatened by Christianity, which was introduced to Japan by Francis Xavier in 1549.

Do I really have to write "I must make money" five hundred times?

Life at the Top

I knew that I was important, even as a child. I knew because I was born into the samurai class, the class of noble warriors. I make sure that all the social classes below me stay in their place. I keep a close eye on ministers in my government, which is called *bakufu*.

I MUST ALWAYS BE AHEAD OF MINISTERS AND COURTIERS. They can be really tricky. Some even want to push me out. I use a network of samurai spies to check on them. If they plot against me, they might be finished off with a tiny dart tipped with a killer poison, expertly mixed by a samurai warrior.

I CRACK DOWN HARD ON FEUDAL LORDS. *I am a very generous shogun and allow feudal lords, called* daimyo, *to control some of my regions. Feudal lords allow peasants to use their land in return for a lot of taxes. Daimyo are ruthless and police their regions harshly. They squabble with one another too. Some of the worst clashes took place in 1490. I keep my army of warriors at the ready to sort them out.*

You could have carried another sack between your teeth! Fetch the guard!

This is a truly smelly skin. The guard won't want to come in here.

I KEEP THE POOR IN THEIR PLACE. *The lower classes must not try to get to the top. These include rice farmers, who live in villages that have to to pay heavy rice taxes. Artisans and craftsmen come next, then fishermen. Merchants are at the bottom. They might have money, but they do not have respect. The underclass includes entertainers, beggars, executioners, and leather workers. Imagine handling rotting carcasses and stinking animal skins for a living!*

Fiendish Fact File

- Bakufu means "tent government" because the first ministers were samurai warriors on the battlefields.

- Shoguns feared peasants after Toyotomi Hideyoshi (1536-1598), a peasant, defeated Japan's generals and became shogun.

- Peasants could be killed on the spot by a samurai for any reason. There were frequent peasant uprisings, or *ikki*, because of harsh taxes, famine, and corruption.

I DO NOT TRUST THOSE FIENDISH PEASANTS! *I must control their movement. I forbid travel across the country except along the Five Highways, which my troops patrol. This stops peasants from organizing rebellions.*

Being a Bad Neighbor

I enjoy fighting, but we have been at peace with my neighbors since the 1590s. This was when Shogun Toyotomi Hideyoshi tried to invade Korea but failed. Never mind. I still have plenty of enemies to watch at home. They range from warlords to bakufu ministers. Tricky people.

I MUST STAMP ON RIVALS to keep peace and calm in Japan. So I often go into battle against rival samurai warlords. My role model is Shogun Oda Nobunaga. He crushed them using peasant armies equipped with firearms. These were introduced by the Portuguese in 1543. But peasant armies can be dangerous to a shogun. So I also admire my ancestor, Toyotomi Hideyoshi, who then disbanded peasant soldiers and abolished firearms.

I WILL NOT ACCEPT OTHER RELIGIONS. Spain's Francis Xavier (1506-1552) brought Christianity here in 1549. He called us "the best people yet discovered." Of course! But a foreign faith could encourage foreign armies and Japan's own Christian peasants to attack me. Or it could challenge our traditional Shinto faith and its leader, the Emperor. What would I do without his support?

I use this for defense, you understand.

14

I MUST NOT BE NICE FOR TOO LONG. This is a very important rule, especially with foreign merchants. At first, I did not mind Portuguese, Dutch, and English trading ships arriving at our shores. But then they started to take trade away from us. I did send in my diplomatic corps, the *buke kaigo* to have a little chat about it. But I soon turned our navy on them.

I REALLY CANNOT PUT UP WITH PIRATES. We call pirates *wako*. These cutthroat enemies plunder the shores of Japan's islands. I ordered the *bakufu* to build many warships. So now these fire cannons that blast pirate ships out of the water. At times our neighbor Korea has helped us out too.

Shame. I like the way pirates think.

Fiendish Fact File

- The most ferocious fighting between the daimyo occurred between 1467 and 1568. This is known as *Sengoku jidai*, the time of civil war.

- Shoguns persecuted Japanese Christians. But in 1637, Christian peasants fought back. They burned Buddhist temples but eventually were crushed.

- In 1633, Japan was closed to the outside world for trade and travel. Then in 1853, US Navy Commodore Matthew Perry arrived in Uraga port and ordered Japan to open up trade.

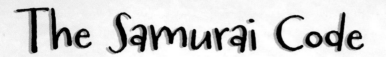

The Samurai Code

Only top-class warriors like me become samurai. In battle we are fiendish both as foot soldiers and cavalry. Our enemies dare not chase us on horseback, for we can turn in our saddles and face them with our razor-sharp weapons.

WE ALL FOLLOW THE STRICT *BUSHIDO* CODE. We begin bushido training when we are only five years old. We learn self-control, bravery, and how to think like a soldier. My samurai must be disciplined, kind, and honorable and respect their parents. They must be loyal to one another and to ME. I insist that samurai live in towns. This stops them from becoming the allies of rebel peasants.

> I'm an excellent role model.

> Remember that I'm killing you kindly, with honor and respect. It'll make all the difference.

Fiendish Fact File

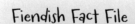

- Ninja's *shuriken* were metal stars that fit in the hand. They could be thrown to spike or slash an opponent or used at close range.

- Ninja knew how to create showers of sparks and clouds of smoke to confuse the enemy.

- *Kenjutsu* is the "way of the sword," or the art of sword fighting. Samurai practiced it with double-edged wooden swords with no sharp edges.

MY SAMURAI MUST BE EXPERT SWORDSMEN. *The main samurai weapon is the* katana. *This is a heavy, curved sword with a very sharp double edge. My samurai use it to slash from left to right or rip upward. But they need to be strong, swift, and supple athletes to kill with the katana.*

I MUST VALUE MY NINJA FIGHTERS. *They are masters of disguise, excellent spies, and quiet as cats. Ninja fight with bows, arrows, swords, and knives. They can kill with blowguns or fight hand-to-hand with brass knuckledusters. Sharp shuriken weapons are hidden in their hands. Unseen, ninja cross raging rivers and climb towering castle walls. This is all good unless my enemies are employing ninja too.*

He's my ninja, and he's come to kill you.

No, he's MY ninja, and he's come to kill YOU!

I MUST KEEP AN EYE ON THE RONIN. *These skilled samurai wander around my country looking for trouble. Many of them served a warlord who died. But some of them misbehaved and lost their warlord's trust. They are often employed by my enemies—and sometimes, by ME. I wish I had ronin Miyamoto Musashi (1584-1645) on my side. He could kill with a simple bamboo sword. But he rarely took a bath or changed his clothes, so maybe I'm not so sure . . .*

So why should I employ you?

I'm an expert at treachery, sabotage, murder . . . what's not to like?

17

My Fiendish Fortress

I must always look powerful and impressive. My towering castle and massive defensive walls at my capital, Edo, do the trick. But there are other great castles in Japan. My bakufu military officials and daimyo regional lords build them too. I must make mine greater than theirs.

ALWAYS LEARN FROM THE PAST. This is the first rule I give my architects. My ancestors' castles were made of earthworks and wood, so they were never going to last long. Catapulted flames, new imported cannons, arquebus (early rifles), and our many earthquakes soon turned them to rubble and ash. Obviously.

Fiendish Fact File

- Oda Nobunaga showed no mercy to men, women, or children under a castle siege. Great catapults hurled burning missiles over the walls. The entire castle complex went up in flames.

- Edo Castle is now the impressive Imperial Palace in Tokyo, the modern capital city of Japan.

I told a tricky warlord that this was the best design. See? I learned from the past.

BUILD IT BIG AND STRONG. My castle is defended by rings of thick stone walls. There are several moats between the walls too. An elegant, pagoda-shaped, multi-story castle rises above them. Inside, my rooms are decorated lavishly with statues of fish, birds, and tigers. I hear that a daimyo at Fushimi Castle has covered the walls of his tearoom with gold leaf. I shall certainly be copying that!

I think it needs just one more story. Or would that be too much?

I MUST FOLLOW MY HERO. Oda Nobunaga was a truly ruthless warlord who supported shoguns. His huge castle at Azuchi became a model for many castles across Japan. Other daimyo feudal lords copied the design and built their castles on vast plains. From there they could control powerful, aggressive warriors. My only problem is this: how can I control a powerful daimyo who refuses to obey ME?

MY CASTLE MUST BE WELL-GUARDED. This is an essential rule. My castle gates are firmly shut at night and guarded by warriors. Half an hour before sunrise, bells clank and ring. They are struck from tall towers in tight, shadowy streets of closely packed rowhouses (*see page 21*). It is now safe to open my gates. The bells also tell my subjects to get up and go to work. An excellent rule.

19

Building My Capital

I must build a capital greater than the Emperor's in Kyoto. This was the plan of the first shogun, Minamoto Yoritomo. He built a new capital in Kamakura, far to the east of Kyoto.

MY CAPITAL MUST BE BETTER THAN YOURS. My capital, Edo, also east of Kyoto, was once a small fishing port. The name Edo means "mouth of the bay." Within my enormous city walls there are Buddhist temples, beautiful gardens, woods, and streams. My mighty fortress sits at the center, rising above a network of bustling streets. Stunning!

20

STOP MY CAPITAL FROM FLOODING! Because Edo is on the coast, it is easily flooded. But I follow the example of the founder of Edo, Shogun Tokugawa Ieyasu. After 1603, he had the land around Edo drained. Canals and irrigation systems were constructed. I keep all these works maintained. My biggest fears are typhoons—and earthquakes!

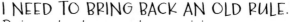

I think we can squeeze a few more houses in here. Plenty of room!

SIMPLE HOMES FOR SIMPLE PEOPLE. My wealthy citizens live in spacious and beautiful wooden homes with garden rooms to relax in. They are arranged in a grid along nice streets. But I tax the poor according to the width of their homes. So they build narrow rowhouses squashed together in tiny alleyways. Shame. Farmers in the country live with their horses and cattle. I expect it keeps them warm.

Fiendish Fact File

- Edo became Tokyo, the modern capital of Japan. Tokyo means "eastern capital"—it lies east of Kyoto.

- Rowhouses were very small. Most were only one story though some were two stories. The lower floor was a shop or other kind of business.

I NEED TO BRING BACK AN OLD RULE. Daimyo lords are always giving me trouble. I need them to come to my capital so I can keep an eye on them. In earlier times, daimyo were weak. They were in charge only of small local governments called *han*. Every other year, the shoguns ordered daimyo to stay in Edo for several months. If they disobeyed, they were killed. So were their families. Sounds like a plan.

I beg you. PLEASE let me out!

Becoming Very Rich

I will only get rich if I gather taxes from the land. I will only stay rich if I keep the peace. Wars disrupt farming and markets and destroy roads and bridges. I must avoid conflict, which is very hard for me.

That's my new gold-papered bedroom crossed off the list.

WE MUST CREATE WEALTH. I will not let Japan remain a poor, feudal, farming nation. So I encourage the mining and smelting of metals. We also manufacture silks and cottons, fine paper, and porcelain china. Our artisans make intricate carvings from fruit woods and ivory. Of course, we export many of these goods. Strangely, I am not able to tax the profits on trade, but my people are more prosperous and happy. That stops them from rioting.

You need another porcelain tea set or you'll riot? Here, take two.

TAX, TAX, TAX. My daimyo get rich on rice taxes. But my government makes sure that the daimyo also spend money on public works. These include building roads, canals, and other irrigation systems. This helps farming, communications, and trade—and makes me look good too.

Look! I've only got one bag left!

SPEND, SPEND, SPEND. This is a great rule, and I spend a lot. But I want my subjects to spend too. It makes Japan very wealthy. Our middle classes are growing quickly. They have lots of spare money, and they complain all the time. So I make sure there are enough luxury goods to keep them happy. These include silk fashion items, jade jewelry, and carved, lacquered handicrafts. So it's shop till you drop in our many stores and markets.

I MUST KEEP AN EYE ON KYOTO. The Emperor's city is worryingly rich. My subjects enjoy shopping there. Some silk shops employ up to five hundred people. Kyoto's streets are teeming with peddlers selling everything from miso, fermented soybean soup, to sticky rice sweets. I like the sweets.

Your favorite rice cake with sweet red anko paste, Your Majesty?

Fiendish Fact File

- Matsuzakaya in Edo was one of the first department stores in the world, set up in 1768 by the Ito family, who were originally samurai.

- Japan's economy, and the cities of Edo, Kyoto, and Osaka, expanded rapidly from the 1680s to the 1700s.

23

My Lavish Lifestyle

Showing off is a very important rule. My palaces must look good, and so must I. Only the finest silk, linen, and leather clothing will do. My weapons are of the best tempered steel. The hilts of my swords are decorated with lacquered gold and copper patterns.

FINE FOODS FOR A SUPER SHOGUN. I, of course, eat rice, which must be polished. The lower classes cook it with the husks. My chefs serve up rare, expensive fish and seafood, egg dishes, and seaweeds in delicate bowls. Beautiful. I make sure that peasants cannot afford to eat the rice they grow. Millet, barley, and wheat are good enough for them, with some peas, beans, and herbs.

> I see a husk! Back to the kitchen with it!

THE PEOPLE MUST SEE MY WEALTH. My courtiers organize a great street procession where I show off my finery. I ride on a palanquin decked with bright silks, accompanied by a long line of courtiers, nobles, artists, and musicians. Doctors come too, to make sure I stay in good shape. My nobles enjoy their riches. But I rarely allow them, or their families, outside the city walls. I need to see what they are up to.

A river of stones can't flood my city. Genius!

I INSIST ON BEAUTY. Beauty is power. My fabulous Zen Buddhist gardens show wealth, culture, and intelligence. I particularly like gardens with curved lines of raked stones that represent a flowing river. Large rocks are dotted along it as symbols of mountains. I believe that I am like a mighty mountain. I sit in the garden to meditate on how I can make even more rules.

PEASANTS MUST LOOK POOR. Most peasants can only afford hemp and cotton kimonos, shorts, and straw sandals. Some of my farmers get very rich though. They can even buy kimonos embroidered with fancy patterns. This worries me. I must tax them more. I never allow daimyo to wear the best silks, but they can wear *eboshi* caps tied on with a white cord.

You all look a bit too smart and well-fed to me.

Maybe just a little exercise might be good for you, Your Highness?

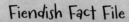

Fiendish Fact File

- We know about the finery of a shogun's court from Dutch and English merchants' eyewitness accounts.

- Peasants made up 80 percent of the population under the shoguns. They paid 60 percent of their crops in taxes.

- Ukiyo-e artists flourished during the Edo period. They became famous for their greeting cards, albums, and wall hangings printed from woodblock designs.

My Powerful Death

I insist on a long and expensive Zen Buddhist funeral to show my power in death. When I die, my body will rest for a few hours or days before it is washed and clothed in fine robes. Nobles, and daimyo from afar, will come to pay their respects. If I die in summer, my body will rest for a short while so it does not stink.

I WILL NOT CUT CORNERS WITH MY FUNERAL. My body will be placed in a coffin and carried to the temple. A fiendish portrait of me will be hung above my head. Golden screens will be placed upside down around me to ward off evil spirits if they dare come close. Then the lid will close down on me. Gorgeous silks will be draped over my coffin. I am ready.

THE KIGAN BUTSUJI PROCESSION MUST BE LONG AND NOISY. My coffin will be ceremonially transported from the temple to the funeral pyre. Family, nobles, daimyo, and the high priest will accompany me. Samurai will march in their finest armor. Boy monks will chant sutras. Beating drums, clashing cymbals, glowing lanterns, waving banners, and wafting incense will give me a good send-off. Spectacular!

Hurry up with the perfume!

I wonder why they're not crying?

I WILL NEED A GOOD FIRE. When we reach the crematorium, a polite tea ceremony will welcome me. Libations, or offerings of water, will be poured around me. The coffin will be placed high on the funeral pyre. Then, the *ako butsuji* (torch-lighting ceremony) will ignite the pyre, and my body will turn to ash. But my spirit will be reborn. I hope I will become a shogun again in the future, not a poor peasant.

> I think there has been a mistake!

NOT SO LUCKY. But what is this? A message from the Emperor says that I am a useless ruler. A rival shogun is ready to take over. My guard hands me a sword to commit seppuku. I must stab myself—and die. But wait! I remember the bushido rule of duty. So I shall dutifully fight this rival shogun. Phew! Long live ME!.

Fiendish Fact File

- The funeral rituals for shogun Ashikaga Yoshimochi (ruled 1395-1428) lasted forty-nine days.

- Shrines were decorated with carvings of the mythical beast, *kirin*. This lion- or horse-like figure, sometimes with wings, was thought to bring peace.

The Way of the Warrior

Shoguns and all other samurai warriors had to follow an eight-point code of conduct called bushido. The code developed during the Kamakura period (1192-1333).

Rectitude—knowing the right time to act and making the right decisions. A samurai needed to know when to strike or even when to die.

Courage—doing what is right! Courage sometimes meant having the strength to say no.

Benevolence and mercy—the highest quality for a samurai leader. This meant love, sympathy, pity, and being generous and gracious when he was wrong.

Politeness—respect for the feelings of other people.

Honesty and sincerity—valuing wisdom over money was the way to stay honest. A samurai could not lower himself by talking about money.

Honor—valuing both the duties and benefits of his position. A samurai would take pride in what he did and not disgrace himself. Honor included patience and calm. A quick temper was not honorable.

Loyalty—to his lord and to the samurai he fought with.

Character and self-control—being strong and keeping to his values, even if they did not seem logical. He knew what was right and kept to it.

THE DARK SIDE OF BUSHIDO

Bushido honor led to seppuku. This was a horrific ritual death. A samurai committed seppuku after defeat in battle or if his lord was murdered. Death was long and painful.

Women from the samurai class committed jigai, a terrible form of seppuku, using a short sword or dagger. In the fifteenth century, female samurai had to fight to defend towns and castles. If they were defeated, they committed jigai.

More Fiendish Shoguns

Here are some more fiendish shoguns and daimyo.
I think I could teach them a few more fiendish rules.

1 Minamoto no Yoriie (ruled 1202–1203) planned to murder his younger brother, Sanetomo, with his father-in-law's help. In the end, both plotters were murdered by rival warriors from the Hojo family. Most fiendish.

2 Ashikaga Yoshinori (ruled 1428–1441) made crazy, ruthless decisions. He forced Ashikaga Mochiuji to kill himself for setting himself up as ruler. Yoshinori himself was assassinated while watching a play.

3 Ashikaga Yoshimasa (ruled 1449–1474) ignored the civil war around him. Instead he had fun building the Silver Pavilion in Kyoto and organizing tea ceremonies. In 1474 he retired, and his son took over.

4 Ashikaga Yoshiharu (ruled 1521–1546) lived in Kyoto but was always being bullied by his foes. In 1542, a Portuguese trading ship came. Yoshiharu received Japan's first European visitors and was famous at last.

5 Ashikaga Yoshiteru (ruled 1546–1565) was respected because of his swordsmanship and for keeping peace in Japan. But Yoshiteru was still murdered by one of his vassal lords. Fiendish.

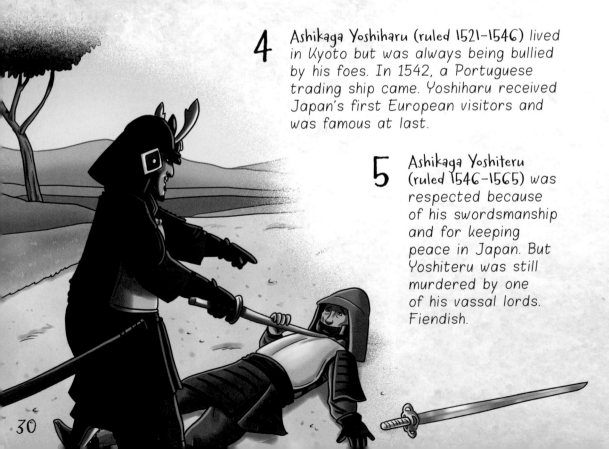

6 Ashikaga Yoshiaki (ruled 1568–1573) kicked out his cousin, Yoshihide, to become the last shogun of the Ashikaga shogunate. He was helped by daimyo warlord Oda Nobunaga.

7 Oda Nobunaga (1534–1582) was a fiendish daimyo. He ended the Ashikaga shogunate and unified half of Japan. But he burned down Buddhist monasteries and besieged castles, killing all inside.

8 Tokugawa Ieyasu (ruled 1603–1616) was the first shogun of the Tokugawa, or Edo, dynasty. In 1615 he attacked Osaka castle, killing all the rival Toyotomi family inside. In Ieyasu's last battle of unification at Sekigahara, 36,000 foes were killed or maimed in one day.

9 Tokugawa Hidetada (ruled 1616–1632) was Ieyasu's son. Like his father, Hidetada thought that Japanese Christians and their Spanish friends would rebel against him. So in 1622 he executed 122 Christians.

10 Tokugawa Tsunayoshi (ruled 1680–1709) loved dogs. Anyone who hurt a dog was executed. Tsunayoshi spent government money on keeping 50,000 dogs. He fed them an expensive diet of fish and rice.

INDEX

The Author

Catherine Chambers was born in Adelaide, South Australia and brought up in England. She earned a degree in African History and Swahili at the School of Oriental and African Studies, London. Catherine has written about 130 titles for children and young adults, mainly non-fiction, and she enjoys seeking out intriguing facts for her non-fiction titles.

The Illustrator

Ryan Pentney lives and works in Norwich, in the United Kingdom. Growing up in the 1990s, he was surrounded by iconic cartoons, comics, and books that have remained a passion with him. Inspired by these childhood heroes as well as more modern works, Ryan creates his own characters and stories in the hope of inspiring the next generation. He uses the latest technology and traditional techniques to make stylized digital artworks.